Clementine A. Fortier

Super Mind boggling crazy facts

This book was professionally typeset on Reedsy
Find out more at reedsy.com

Contents

1.

2.

3.

4.

5.

6.

7.

8.

9.

10.

11.

I
Part One

1

Introduction

Step into a world where the ordinary transforms into the extraordinary, and curiosity becomes your guide. "Super Mind-Boggling Facts for Curious People: Mind-Blowing Facts" is not just a book; it's a journey through the marvels of our universe that will leave your mind racing and your sense of wonder rekindled. Prepare to be captivated by a collection of the most astonishing, jaw-dropping, and downright mind-bending facts that will challenge everything you thought you knew.

As you flip through the pages of this book, you'll uncover secrets hidden in plain sight and unravel mysteries that defy logic. Did you know that honey never spoils and has been found in ancient Egyptian tombs still perfectly edible? Or that there's a species of jellyfish capable of reverting its cells to infancy, effectively aging backward? These are just a glimpse into the realm of super mind-boggling facts awaiting you.

Each page is a portal to a new revelation, a discovery that will ignite your imagination and leave you craving more. From the depths of the ocean to the vastness of space, embark on a voyage of knowledge that transcends the boundaries of the known and embraces the limitless wonders that surround us.

But this isn't just a collection of random facts; it's a carefully curated experience designed to tickle your intellect and spark conversations. Share these mind-blowing revelations with friends, family, and colleagues, and watch as discussions light up with amazement.

Are you ready to embark on a journey that will challenge the limits of your understanding and expand the horizons of your knowledge? Click the "Buy Now" button and let the adventure begin. Super Mind-Boggling Facts for Curious People is not just a book; it's an invitation to explore the extraordinary in the ordinary, a ticket to a world where the only limit is the extent of your curiosity.

2

Animals

1. Honeybees can recognize human faces.
2. The mimic octopus can imitate the appearance and behaviors of other marine species.
3. Elephants are the only mammals that can't jump.
4. Cows have best friends and can become stressed when separated from them.
5. A group of flamingos is called a "flamboyance."
6. The tongue of a blue whale can weigh as much as an elephant.
7. The narwhal's long tusk is actually an elongated tooth.
8. The cheetah is the fastest land animal, capable of reaching speeds up to 75 mph.
9. The heart of a shrimp is located in its head.
10. Star-nosed moles can eat food faster than the human eye can follow.
11. Oysters can change their gender depending on the environment.
12. The longest recorded flight of a chicken is 13 seconds.
13. Sloths take two weeks to digest their food.
14. A newborn kangaroo is about 1 inch in length.
15. A single strand of spider silk is stronger than steel.
16. Cats have five toes on their front paws but only four on their back paws.
17. A giraffe's tongue can be up to 45 cm long.
18. The only mammal capable of flight is the bat.
19. A snail can sleep for three years.
20. A group of owls is called a "parliament."
21. A shrimp's heart is located in its head.
22. Some birds are capable of recognizing themselves in a mirror.
23. The archer fish can spit water up to 5 feet to catch prey.
24. A male seahorse carries and gives birth to the babies.
25. Axolotls can regenerate their limbs and even parts of their heart and brain.
26. A group of crows is called a "murder."
27. The tongue of a chameleon is twice the length of its body.
28. The only mammal capable of flight is the bat.
29. A group of jellyfish is called a "smack."

30. The bombardier beetle can spray boiling chemicals at its predators.

31. Cats have a unique fingerprint – the pattern on their nose is distinctive.

32. The elephant is the only mammal that can't jump.

33. The fingerprints of a koala are so indistinguishable from humans that they have, on occasion, been confused at a crime scene.

34. A newborn kangaroo is about 1 inch in length.

35. A group of ferrets is called a "business."

36. The basilisk lizard can run on water to escape predators.

37. The color of a flamingo's feathers is influenced by its diet.

38. The slowest mammal is the three-toed sloth, which moves at a speed of 0.03 mph.

39. The largest living structure on Earth is the Great Barrier Reef, built by corals.

40. The electric eel can produce shocks of up to 600 volts.

41. The quokka is known as the "happiest" animal due to its smiling appearance.

42. Pigeons can recognize themselves in a mirror.

43. The star-nosed mole can identify and consume prey in less than a quarter of a second.

44. A group of ravens is called an "unkindness."

45. A shrimp's heart is located in its head.

46. The tongue of a blue whale can weigh as much as an elephant.

47. A newborn kangaroo is about 1 inch in length.

48. Cows have best friends and can become stressed when separated from them.

49. The mimic octopus can imitate the appearance and behaviors of other marine species.

50. Honeybees can recognize human faces.

51. A group of flamingos is called a "flamboyance."

52. The narwhal's long tusk is actually an elongated tooth.

53. The cheetah is the fastest land animal, capable of reaching speeds up to 75 mph.

54. The heart of a shrimp is located in its head.

55. Star-nosed moles can eat food faster than the human eye can follow.

56. Oysters can change their gender depending on the environment.

57. The longest recorded flight of a chicken is 13 seconds.

58. Sloths take two weeks to digest their food.

59. A newborn kangaroo is about 1 inch in length.

60. A single strand of spider silk is stronger than steel.

61. Cats have five toes on their front paws but only four on their back paws.

62. A giraffe's tongue can be up to 45 cm long.

63. The only mammal capable of flight is the bat.

64. A snail can sleep for three years.

65. A group of owls is called a "parliament."

66. A shrimp's heart is located in its head.

67. Some birds are capable of recognizing themselves in a mirror.

68. The archer fish can spit water up to 5 feet to catch prey.

69. A male seahorse carries and gives birth to the babies.

70. Axolotls can regenerate their limbs and even parts of their heart and brain.

3

Science

1. The Earth is about 4.54 billion years old.
2. Honey never spoils; archaeologists have found pots of honey in ancient Egyptian tombs that are over 3,000 years old and still perfectly edible.
3. The total length of DNA in the human body is approximately 2 meters.
4. A teaspoonful of neutron star material would weigh about 6 billion tons on Earth.
5. There are more possible iterations of a game of chess than there are atoms in the observable universe.
6. The speed of light is approximately 299,792 kilometers per second (186,282 miles per second).
7. There are more microbes in one teaspoon of soil than there are people on Earth.
8. Every element on the periodic table was formed within a star.
9. The human brain can generate about 20 watts of electrical power.
10. The largest volcano in our solar system is on Mars, called Olympus Mons.
11. One tablespoon of a neutron star would weigh about 6 billion tons.
12. The most abundant gas in the Earth's atmosphere is nitrogen, making up about 78%.
13. A day on Venus is longer than a year on Venus.
14. The shortest war in history was between Britain and Zanzibar on August 27, 1896, lasting only 38 minutes.
15. Octopuses have three hearts.
16. The first image of a black hole was captured in 2019 by the Event Horizon Telescope.
17. The universe is expanding, and galaxies are moving away from each other.
18. Cows have best friends and can become stressed when they are separated.
19. The world's largest desert is Antarctica.
20. The smallest bone in the human body is the stapes bone in the ear.
21. The Eiffel Tower can be 15 cm taller during the summer due to thermal expansion.
22. A single rainforest can produce 20% of the Earth's oxygen.
23. The human body contains enough iron to make a 3-inch nail.

24. The coldest temperature ever recorded on Earth was minus 128.6 degrees Fahrenheit (-89.2 degrees Celsius) in Antarctica.

25. There are more stars in the universe than grains of sand on all the beaches on Earth.

26. A teaspoonful of a neutron star would weigh as much as a mountain on Earth.

27. The average person walks the equivalent of three times around the world in their lifetime.

28. The Great Wall of China is not visible from the Moon with the naked eye.

29. The smell of freshly-cut grass is actually a plant distress call.

30. The Earth's core is as hot as the surface of the Sun.

31. Bananas are berries, but strawberries are not.

32. A day on Mercury is longer than its year.

33. The human eye can distinguish about 10 million different colors.

34. The Great Barrier Reef is the largest living structure on Earth.

35. There are more possible iterations of a deck of cards than there are atoms on Earth.

36. Water can exist in three states simultaneously - solid, liquid, and gas - at the triple point.

37. The Sun loses about 4 million tons of mass every second due to nuclear fusion.

38. The longest time between two twins being born is 87 days.

39. The world's oceans contain nearly 20 million tons of gold.

40. A neutron star can spin up to 600 times per second.

41. The first computer programmer was a woman named Ada Lovelace.

42. The shortest war in history lasted only 2 hours and 30 minutes between Britain and Zanzibar in 1896.

43. There are more bacteria in a person's mouth than there are people in the world.

44. A single rainforest can produce 20% of the Earth's oxygen.

45. The largest living organism on Earth is a fungus in Oregon's Malheur National Forest.

46. A day on Pluto is equivalent to about 153 hours on Earth.

47. The human brain can process information as fast as 120 meters per second.

48. Only 5% of the universe is made up of ordinary matter; the rest is dark matter and dark energy.

49. The largest volcano in the solar system is on Mars, named Olympus Mons.

50. The Andromeda Galaxy is on a collision course with our Milky Way galaxy and will merge in about 4 billion years.

4

Sports

The first recorded evidence of organized sports dates back to 3000 BC in Egypt.

Cricket is one of the oldest known sports, with origins tracing back to the 16th century.

The first Olympic Games were held in Olympia, Greece, in 776 BC.

The modern Olympics were revived in 1896 in Athens, Greece.

The official sport of Maryland, USA, is jousting.

The longest tennis match in history lasted 11 hours and 5 minutes.

The fastest tennis serve ever recorded was at 163.7 mph by Sam Groth.

Wilt Chamberlain scored 100 points in a single NBA game in 1962.

The first hockey pucks were made of cow dung.

Table tennis is the most popular racquet sport globally.

The first official game of basketball was played with a soccer ball and two peach baskets.

The average golf ball has 336 dimples.

The first recorded women's bowling league was established in 1917.

Baseball umpires used to sit in rocking chairs during games in the 19th century.

The most expensive baseball card ever sold was a Honus Wagner card for $3.12 million.

The longest recorded golf drive is 515 yards by Michael Hoke Austin.

Muhammad Ali won a gold medal in boxing at the 1960 Olympics.

The fastest knockout in boxing history was 1.9 seconds.

The only sport ever played on the moon is golf.

The first recorded game of American football was played in 1869.

A professional soccer player runs an average of 7 miles per game.

The oldest soccer ball ever discovered is over 450 years old.

The fastest goal in soccer history was scored in 2.8 seconds.

Michael Phelps holds the record for the most Olympic gold medals in swimming.

The first World Series in baseball was played in 1903.

The most-watched sporting event in the world is the FIFA World Cup.

The highest score in a single game of Scrabble is 365 points.

Chess is the oldest known board game, with origins dating back to the 6th century.

The first recorded marathon took place in 490 BC, run by Pheidippides.

Golf is the only sport to have been played on the moon.

The most expensive sports stadium ever built is the MetLife Stadium, costing $1.6 billion.

The first official international cricket match was played between the United States and Canada in 1844.

The longest recorded game of Monopoly lasted for 70 days.

The longest recorded snooker match lasted for 77 hours and 46 minutes.

The first game of modern rugby was played in 1823 when a player picked up the ball during a soccer game.

The first official game of baseball was played in 1846.

The longest field goal in NFL history is 64 yards.

The fastest hat trick in soccer was scored in 70 seconds.

The first official hockey game was played in 1875 in Montreal.

The oldest known sport still played today is wrestling.

Jai alai is the fastest ball game in the world, with balls reaching speeds of 188 mph.

The highest-scoring NBA game in history was 186-184.

The most points scored by a single player in an NBA game is 100 points by Wilt Chamberlain.

The first recorded game of golf was played in 1457 in Scotland.

The first official women's basketball game was played in 1892.

The first recorded game of badminton was played in India in the mid-19th century.

The largest sports stadium in the world is the Rungrado 1st of May Stadium in North Korea.

The first recorded game of table tennis was played in England in 1884.

The first women's cricket match was played in 1745.

The most expensive sports memorabilia ever sold is a 1920 Babe Ruth jersey for $5.64 million.

The first recorded game of curling was played in Scotland in 1541.

The first official game of ice hockey was played in 1875.

The fastest land animal, the cheetah, can reach speeds of 75 mph.

The first recorded game of field hockey was played in 1352.

The highest-scoring game in NBA history was 186-184.

The first recorded game of lacrosse was played by Native Americans in the 17th century.

The first recorded game of volleyball was played in 1895.

The first recorded game of handball was played in 1897.

The first recorded game of rugby sevens was played in 1883.

The first recorded game of polo was played in Persia in the 6th century BC.

The first recorded game of squash was played in England in the 19th century.

The first recorded game of water polo was played in 1876.

The first recorded game of modern pentathlon was played in 1912.

The first recorded game of surfing was in Polynesia in the 18th century.

The first recorded game of bobsleigh was played in Switzerland in the late 19th century.

The first recorded game of skeleton was played in Switzerland in the late 19th century.

The first recorded game of synchronized swimming was played in the early 20th century.

The first recorded game of roller derby was played in 1935.

The first recorded game of ultimate frisbee was played in 1968.

The first recorded game of parkour was played in France in the 20th century.

These facts span a wide range of sports and their fascinating histories!

5

space wonders:

Step into a world where the ordinary transforms into the extraordinary, and curiosity becomes your guide. "Super Mind-Boggling Facts for Curious People: Mind-Blowing Facts" is not just a book; it's a journey through the marvels of our universe that will leave your mind racing and your sense of wonder rekindled. Prepare to be captivated by a collection of the most astonishing, jaw-dropping, and downright mind-bending facts that will challenge everything you thought you knew.

As you flip through the pages of this book, you'll uncover secrets hidden in plain sight and unravel mysteries that defy logic. Did you know that honey never spoils and has been found in ancient Egyptian tombs still perfectly edible? Or that there's a species of jellyfish capable of reverting its cells to infancy, effectively aging backward? These are just a glimpse into the realm of super mind-boggling facts awaiting you.

Each page is a portal to a new revelation, a discovery that will ignite your imagination and leave you craving more. From the depths of the ocean to the vastness of space, embark on a voyage of knowledge that transcends the boundaries of the known and embraces the limitless wonders that surround us.

But this isn't just a collection of random facts; it's a carefully curated experience designed to tickle your intellect and spark conversations. Share these mind-blowing revelations with friends, family, and colleagues, and watch as discussions light up with amazement.

Are you ready to embark on a journey that will challenge the limits of your understanding and expand the horizons of your knowledge? Click the "Buy Now" button and let the adventure begin. Super Mind-Boggling Facts for Curious People is not just a book; it's an invitation to explore the extraordinary in the ordinary, a ticket to a world where the only limit is the extent of your curiosity.

6

Invention

The wheel, one of the earliest inventions, dates back to around 3500 BC.

The first recorded use of a compass for navigation was in China during the Han Dynasty around 206 BC.

The printing press, invented by Johannes Gutenberg around 1440, revolutionized the spread of information.

The first known alarm clock was created by the Greek engineer Ctesibius in the 3rd century BC.

The pencil with an eraser was patented in 1858 by Hyman Lipman, combining two essential writing tools.

Benjamin Franklin invented bifocals in 1784, allowing people to see both near and far.

The first practical telephone was invented by Alexander Graham Bell in 1876.

The first successful demonstration of television occurred in 1927 by Philo Farnsworth.

Velcro was inspired by burrs sticking to clothing and was invented in 1948 by George de Mestral.

Microwave ovens were developed accidentally during World War II when radar technology was being researched.

The concept of the computer mouse was introduced by Douglas Engelbart in 1964.

The barcode, used for product identification, was invented in 1952 by Joseph Woodland and Bernard Silver.

The first computer, ENIAC, was completed in 1945 and occupied a room about 30 by 50 feet in size.

The World Wide Web was invented by Sir Tim Berners-Lee in 1989.

The first digital camera was created by Steven Sasson at Kodak in 1975, weighing around 8 pounds.

The Post-it Note was invented by Arthur Fry and Spencer Silver in 1974.

The Frisbee was accidentally invented by Walter Morrison in 1938 when he threw a pie tin.

The pacemaker, a device for regulating heartbeats, was invented in 1958 by Wilson Greatbatch.

The first successful organ transplant, a kidney, was performed in 1954 by Dr. Joseph Murray.

The disposable razor was invented by King C. Gillette in 1901.

The concept of 3D printing dates back to the 1980s, but it gained popularity in recent years.

The first video game, "Tennis for Two," was created in 1958 by physicist William Higinbotham.

The concept of email was developed by Ray Tomlinson in 1971.

The ballpoint pen was invented by Laszlo Biro in 1938.

The first successful open-heart surgery was performed by Dr. John Gibbon in 1953.

The Segway, a personal transportation device, was invented by Dean Kamen in 2001.

The first successful vaccine was developed by Edward Jenner in 1796 for smallpox.

The artificial heart was invented by Paul Winchell and Dr. Henry Heimlich in 1963.

The MRI (Magnetic Resonance Imaging) machine was invented by Raymond Damadian in the 1970s.

The concept of virtual reality was coined by Jaron Lanier in the 1980s.

The first commercially successful typewriter was invented by Christopher Latham Sholes in 1867.

The modern fire extinguisher was invented by George William Manby in 1813.

The Slinky was accidentally invented by Richard James in 1943 while he was working with springs.

The first electric car was built in the 1830s by Thomas Davenport.

The concept of GPS was developed by the U.S. Department of Defense in the 1970s.

The first practical refrigerator was invented by Carl von Linde in 1876.

The concept of the Internet of Things (IoT) began gaining traction in the late 20th century.

The wind-up clock was invented by Peter Henlein in the 16th century.

The first successful test-tube baby, Louise Brown, was born in 1978 through in vitro fertilization.

The concept of laser technology was theorized by Albert Einstein in 1917.

The first commercial jet airliner, the de Havilland Comet, began service in 1952.

The concept of the helicopter dates back to the 15th century with designs by Leonardo da Vinci.

The first computer virus, the Creeper, was created in the early 1970s.

The concept of the barcode scanner was introduced in the 1970s for retail purposes.

The first patent for a modern airbag was issued to John W. Hetrick in 1953.

The concept of the pacemaker for the heart was developed by Earl Bakken in 1957.

The first commercially successful artificial sweetener, saccharin, was discovered in 1879.

The concept of the electric car dates back to the 19th century with inventors like Thomas Edison.

The first successful kidney transplant was performed in 1954 by Dr. Joseph Murray.

The first successful in vitro fertilization (IVF) was conducted by Patrick Steptoe and Robert Edwards in 1978.

The concept of the space shuttle was developed in the 1960s and first launched in 1981.

The concept of the Segway was introduced by Dean Kamen in 2001.

The first successful cochlear implant was developed in the 1960s by William House.

The concept of CRISPR gene editing technology was developed in the 2010s.

The first practical sewing machine was invented by Elias Howe in 1846.

The concept of the electric guitar was developed in the 1930s.

The first commercially available computer, the UNIVAC I, was delivered in 1951.

The concept of the jet engine was developed independently by Frank Whittle and Hans von Ohain in the 1930s.

The first successful heart transplant was performed by Dr. Christiaan Barnard in 1967.

The concept of the modern bicycle was developed in the 19th century.

The first commercially available computer mouse was developed by Douglas Engelbart in 1968.

The concept of the pacemaker for the heart was developed by Wilson Greatbatch in 1958.

The first successful artificial heart transplant was performed in 1982 by Dr. Barney Clark.

The concept of the electric toothbrush was developed in the 1930s.

The first successful liver transplant was performed in 1967 by Dr. Thomas Starzl.

The concept of the escalator was developed in the late 19th century.

The first commercially successful lithium-ion battery was developed by John B. Goodenough in the 1980s.

The concept of the pacemaker for the heart was developed by Rune Elmqvist and Åke Senning in the 1950s.

The first successful artificial heart transplant was performed in 1982 by Dr. William DeVries.

The concept of the robotic vacuum cleaner was introduced in the 1990s.

7

History

The oldest known written language is Sumerian, dating back to around 3200 BC in Mesopotamia.

Cleopatra, the last pharaoh of Egypt, lived closer in time to the moon landing than to the construction of the Great Pyramid of Giza.

The ancient city of Rome had public toilets with a communal sponge stick for hygiene, shared by multiple people.

The Great Wall of China is not visible from the moon with the naked eye, contrary to popular belief.

The Library of Alexandria, one of the largest and most significant libraries of the ancient world, was destroyed in multiple incidents over centuries, and its exact location remains a mystery.

The word "assassin" is derived from the Arabic word "hashshashin," referring to a secretive medieval group who carried out political murders.

During the Middle Ages, spices such as pepper were so valuable that they were used as currency and could be as valuable as gold.

The shortest war in history was between Britain and Zanzibar in 1896, lasting only 38 minutes.

The Great Fire of London in 1666 was so intense that it melted lead roof tiles and even some of the city's bells.

The Trojan Horse, a giant wooden horse used by the Greeks to infiltrate Troy, is part of Greek mythology and might not have been a historical event.

The Aztecs used cocoa beans as currency, and their emperor, Montezuma II, reportedly drank up to 50 cups of chocolate a day.

The French guillotine, a device for carrying out executions by beheading, was used until 1977.

The phrase "Let them eat cake" is often attributed to Marie Antoinette, but there is no evidence she ever said it.

Ancient Egyptians used a form of toothpaste made from ox hooves, myrrh, and burned eggshells.

The first recorded Olympic Games took place in 776 BC in Olympia, Greece, and featured events such as chariot racing and wrestling.

The longest-reigning monarch in history is Queen Elizabeth II, who has been on the throne since 1952.

The concept of zero was developed by the ancient Maya civilization in Mesoamerica.

The Great Emu War in Australia in 1932 saw the government use machine guns to combat an overpopulation of emus.

The earliest known map dates back to 6th-century Babylon and is carved onto a clay tablet.

The first recorded use of biological warfare occurred in the 14th century when Mongols catapulted plague-infected corpses into the city of Caffa.

The term "barbarian" originally referred to non-Greek speakers, and the Greeks believed their language sounded like "bar-bar."

The city of Istanbul was formerly known as Byzantium and later as Constantinople before being renamed in 1930.

The Spanish Flu of 1918 infected about one-third of the global population and caused an estimated 50 million deaths.

The Eiffel Tower was initially criticized by some of France's leading artists and intellectuals for its design.

The concept of democracy was first introduced in ancient Athens in the 5th century BC.

The word "nerd" was first coined by Dr. Seuss in "If I Ran the Zoo" in 1950.

The Great Depression led to an unusual crime spike, with an increase in bank robberies and thefts.

The first photograph ever taken was by Joseph Nicéphore Niépce in 1826, capturing a view from his window.

The world's oldest known surviving document is the Sumerian "Kish tablet," dating back to around 3500 BC.

The concept of time zones was first proposed by Sir Sandford Fleming at the International Meridian Conference in 1884.

The Huns, led by Attila, invaded Europe in the 5th century, causing widespread panic and migration of various tribes.

The Rosetta Stone, discovered in 1799, played a crucial role in deciphering ancient Egyptian hieroglyphs.

The RMS Titanic sank in 1912, and its wreck was discovered in 1985 by a Franco-American expedition.

The Great Pyramid of Giza originally had a smooth, white limestone casing that reflected the sun's light.

The first recorded use of the term "selfie" dates back to 2002 in an Australian internet forum.

The Battle of Cannae in 216 BC is considered one of the greatest tactical masterpieces, with Hannibal defeating a much larger Roman army.

The concept of the modern calendar was introduced by Pope Gregory XIII in 1582, resulting in the adoption of the Gregorian calendar.

The Berlin Wall, which divided East and West Berlin during the Cold War, fell in 1989, leading to the reunification of Germany.

The Ming Dynasty in China used porcelain pillows to keep heads cool during sleep.

The city of Rome was built on seven hills: Aventine, Caelian, Capitoline, Esquiline, Palatine, Quirinal, and Viminal.

The concept of human rights dates back to ancient civilizations, with the Code of Ur-Nammu in Mesopotamia being one of the earliest examples.

The Industrial Revolution, which began in the 18th century, marked a significant shift from agrarian and handcraft-based economies to industrial and machine-based production.

The Battle of Thermopylae in 480 BC saw a small Greek force, led by King Leonidas I, valiantly resisting the much larger Persian army.

The first recorded joke dates back to Sumerians in 1900 BC and was a proverb about farting.

The Great Famine in Ireland in the mid-19th century led to the death or emigration of millions due to potato crop failures.

The ancient city of Carthage was a powerful rival to Rome, and their conflicts, such as the Punic Wars, shaped Mediterranean history.

The concept of the internet was proposed by J.C.R. Licklider in 1962, envisioning a globally interconnected set of computers.

The concept of "checks and balances" in government was articulated by French political philosopher Montesquieu in the 18th century.

The city of Pompeii was preserved in ash after the eruption of Mount Vesuvius in 79 AD, providing a remarkable snapshot of ancient Roman life.

The first successful human heart transplant was performed by Dr. Christiaan Barnard in South Africa in 1967.

The Black Death in the 14th century killed an estimated 75-200 million people in Eurasia, dramatically altering social and economic structures.

The Gutenberg Bible, printed by Johannes Gutenberg in the 15th century, marked the beginning of the age of the printed book.

The Treaty of Versailles, signed in 1919, officially ended World War I and imposed heavy penalties on Germany, contributing to the rise of Nazism.

The Hanging Gardens of Babylon, one of the Seven Wonders of the Ancient World, may not have existed, as there is no archaeological evidence of their location.

The concept of DNA as the hereditary material was proposed by James Watson and Francis Crick in 1953.

The Silk Road, a network of trade routes connecting the East and West, played a crucial role in cultural exchange and the spread of goods.

The Apollo 11 mission, in 1969, marked the first time humans set foot on the moon, with Neil Armstrong and Buzz Aldrin taking historic steps.

The Battle of Hastings in 1066, led by William the Conqueror, marked the Norman conquest of England.

The Great Sphinx of Giza is believed to have been built during the reign of Pharaoh Khafre around 2500 BC.

The concept of the scientific method was formulated by Sir Francis Bacon in the 17th century.

The concept of democracy in ancient Greece excluded women, slaves, and foreigners from political participation.

The first recorded use of the word "computer" was in reference to a human job title in the 17th century.

The Spanish conquistadors introduced smallpox to the Americas, causing devastating epidemics among indigenous populations.

The Treaty of Westphalia in 1648 marked the end of the Thirty Years' War and is considered a foundational event in modern state sovereignty.

The Great Chicago Fire of 1871, often attributed to Mrs. O'Leary's cow, led to widespread destruction and urban planning reforms.

The concept of the "Iron Curtain" was coined by Winston Churchill to describe the division between Western and Eastern Europe during the Cold War.

The 1913 Women's Suffrage Parade in Washington, D.C., was a pivotal event in the American suffrage movement.

The concept of the steam engine was developed by Thomas Newcomen in the 18th century, laying the foundation for the Industrial Revolution.

The fall of Constantinople in 1453 marked the end of the Byzantine Empire and the beginning of the Renaissance in Europe.

The concept of the "butterfly effect" in chaos theory suggests that small changes can have far-reaching and unpredictable consequences.

8

Pop culture

1. The term "pop culture" originated in the 19th century and was originally associated with the culture of the lower classes.

2. The Beatles' "Sgt. Pepper's Lonely Hearts Club Band" is often considered one of the first concept albums in pop music history.

3. Michael Jackson's "Thriller" is the best-selling album of all time, with over 66 million copies sold worldwide.

4. The term "meme" was coined by British evolutionary biologist Richard Dawkins in 1976.

5. The first video ever played on MTV was "Video Killed the Radio Star" by The Buggles.

6. The iconic "Keep Calm and Carry On" poster originated in Britain during World War II but gained popularity in the 21st century as a meme.

7. The word "selfie" was officially added to the Oxford English Dictionary in 2013.

8. The concept of cosplay (costume play) originated in Japan in the 1970s.

9. The phrase "May the Force be with you" from Star Wars has become a widely recognized pop culture catchphrase.

10. The Simpsons holds the record as the longest-running animated TV series in the world.

11. The term "fan fiction" refers to stories written by fans using characters from existing works.

12. The first known video game, "Tennis for Two," was created in 1958 by physicist William Higinbotham.

13. The term "nerd" was first coined by Dr. Seuss in his book "If I Ran the Zoo."

14. The character of Sherlock Holmes has been portrayed in film and television over 250 times, making it the most portrayed literary human character.

15. "Gangnam Style" by Psy became the first YouTube video to reach one billion views.

16. The phrase "YOLO" (You Only Live Once) gained popularity after being used in Drake's song "The Motto."

17. The term "binge-watch" was officially added to the Oxford English Dictionary in 2013.

18. The first emoji was created in 1999 by Shigetaka Kurita, a Japanese artist.

19. The iconic red-soled shoes of Christian Louboutin have become a symbol of luxury and fashion.

20. The term "blog" is a contraction of the words "web" and "log" and was coined in 1997.

21. The Guinness World Record for the most retweeted tweet is held by a tweet from Carter Wilkerson, who asked for free Wendy's chicken nuggets.

22. The term "hipster" originated in the 1940s and was used to describe jazz enthusiasts.

23. The first known use of the hashtag symbol on social media was by Chris Messina on Twitter in 2007.

24. The iconic "I Love NY" logo was created by graphic designer Milton Glaser in 1977.

25. The word "podcast" is a combination of "iPod" and "broadcast" and was first suggested by journalist Ben Hammersley in 2004.

26. The first-ever computer-generated feature film was "Toy Story," released by Pixar in 1995.

27. The term "clickbait" refers to online content designed to attract attention and encourage users to click on a link.

28. The phrase "Netflix and chill" originated from the idea of casually watching Netflix with someone as a pretext for romantic activity.

29. The concept of virtual reality dates back to the 1960s, but it gained popularity in the 21st century with devices like Oculus Rift.

30. The term "fandom" refers to a subculture of fans who are highly dedicated to a particular work or genre.

31. The first-ever comic book, "The Adventures of Obadiah Oldbuck," was published in 1837.

32. The term "rock 'n' roll" was popularized by DJ Alan Freed in the early 1950s.

33. The concept of the "selfie stick" dates back to the 1980s, but it gained widespread use in the 21st century.

34. The term "emo" is short for "emotional hardcore" and originated in the 1980s punk music scene.

35. The iconic "Star Wars" opening crawl was inspired by the Flash Gordon serials of the 1930s.

36. The first-ever music video aired on MTV was "Video Killed the Radio Star" by
    The Buggles.
37. The term "mashup" refers to a musical genre that combines elements from
    different songs.
38. The phrase "The cake is a lie" became popular in internet culture after its use in
    the video game Portal.
39. The first-ever commercially successful video game was "Pong," released by Atari
    in 1972.
40. The concept of the "man cave" gained popularity in the early 2000s as a dedicated
    space for men in the home.
41. The term "YOLO" gained popularity after being used in Drake's song "The
    Motto."
42. The first-ever emoji was created in 1999 by Shigetaka Kurita, a Japanese artist.
43. The term "hipster" originated in the 1940s and was used to describe jazz
    enthusiasts.
44. The Guinness World Record for the most retweeted tweet is held by a tweet from
    Carter Wilkerson, who asked for free Wendy's chicken nuggets.
45. The term "blog" is a contraction of the words "web" and "log" and was coined in
    1997.
46. The iconic red-soled shoes of Christian Louboutin have become a symbol of
    luxury and fashion.
47. The term "binge-watch" was officially added to the Oxford English Dictionary in
    2013.
48. The first-known use of the hashtag symbol on social media was by Chris Messina
    on Twitter in 2007.
49. The iconic "I Love NY" logo was created by graphic designer Milton Glaser in
    1977.
50. The word "podcast" is a combination of "iPod" and "broadcast" and was first
    suggested by journalist Ben Hammersley in 2004.
51. The first-ever computer-generated feature film was "Toy Story," released by
    Pixar in 1995.
52. The term "clickbait" refers to online content designed to attract attention and
    encourage users to click on a link.
53. The phrase "Netflix and chill" originated from the idea of casually watching
    Netflix with someone as a pretext for romantic activity.
54. The concept of virtual reality dates back to the 1960s, but it gained popularity in
    the 21st century with devices like Oculus Rift.

55. The term "fandom" refers to a subculture of fans who are highly dedicated to a particular work or genre.

56. The first-ever comic book, "The Adventures of Obadiah Oldbuck," was published in 1837.

57. The term "rock 'n' roll" was popularized by DJ Alan Freed in the early 1950s.

58. The concept of the "selfie stick" dates back to the 1980s, but it gained widespread use in the 21st century.

59. The term "emo" is short for "emotional hardcore" and originated in the 1980s punk music scene.

60. The iconic "Star Wars" opening crawl was inspired by the Flash Gordon serials of the 1930s.

61. The first-ever music video aired on MTV was "Video Killed the Radio Star" by The Buggles.

62. The term "mashup" refers to a musical genre that combines elements from different songs.

63. The phrase "The cake is a lie" became popular in internet culture after its use in the video game Portal.

64. The first-ever commercially successful video game was "Pong," released by Atari in 1972.

65. The concept of the "man cave" gained popularity in the early 2000s as a dedicated space for men in the home.

66. The term "YOLO" gained popularity after being used in Drake's song "The Motto."

67. The first-ever emoji was created in 1999 by Shigetaka Kurita, a Japanese artist.

68. The term "hipster" originated in the 1940s and was used to describe jazz enthusiasts.

69. The Guinness World Record for the most retweeted tweet is held by a tweet from Carter Wilkerson, who asked for free Wendy's chicken nuggets.

70. The term "blog" is a contraction of the words "web" and "log" and was coined in 1997

9

Countries

1. Canada has more lakes than the rest of the world combined.

2. The Great Wall of China is not visible from the moon without aid.

3. Australia is the only continent without an active volcano.

4. The Maldives is the lowest country in the world.

5. Sweden has the most islands among all countries.

6. The world's largest desert is Antarctica.

7. Russia spans 11 time zones.

8. Madagascar is home to 5% of the world's plant and animal species.

9. Brazil is named after the Brazilwood tree, not the country.

10. Greenland is the world's largest island but the least densely populated place on Earth.

11. Iran has one of the world's oldest continuous civilizations.

12. The Vatican City is the smallest independent state in the world.

13. Japan experiences around 1,500 earthquakes annually.

14. The highest point in Africa is Mount Kilimanjaro.

15. India is the birthplace of four major religions: Hinduism, Buddhism, Jainism, and Sikhism.

16. New Zealand has more sheep than people.

17. Norway is home to the Midnight Sun phenomenon.

18. Mount Everest is the world's highest peak, located in Nepal.

19. Switzerland is known for its efficient and punctual train system.

20. Bhutan is the only country in the world to measure success in Gross National Happiness.

21. Egypt is home to the ancient Pyramids of Giza.

22. The Amazon Rainforest produces 20% of the world's oxygen.

23. Finland has the highest coffee consumption per capita in the world.

24. Turkey is the only country that is on two continents, Europe and Asia.

25. The United States has the world's longest road network.

26. Indonesia has the most active volcanoes in the world.

27. South Korea has the world's fastest internet speed.

28. Mexico introduced chocolate, chilies, and corn to the world.

29. France is the most visited country in the world.

30. Argentina is home to the world's widest avenue, Avenida 9 de Julio.

31. The Philippines has the highest SMS (text messaging) traffic per capita.

32. Iceland has no mosquitoes.

33. South Africa is the only country to have three capital cities: Pretoria, Cape Town, and Bloemfontein.

34. The Netherlands is one of the world's largest exporters of cheese and flowers.

35. Saudi Arabia has no rivers.

36. The Great Barrier Reef in Australia is the largest living structure on Earth.

37. Peru has the world's highest sand dune, Cerro Blanco.

38. China is the world's largest exporter.

39. Germany is known for its Autobahn, a highway system with no general speed limit.

40. Kenya is home to the Maasai Mara National Reserve.

41. Nepal has 8 of the world's 14 highest peaks, including Mount Everest.

42. Thailand has the world's longest-reigning monarch, King Bhumibol Adulyadej.

43. Spain has the second-highest number of UNESCO World Heritage Sites.

44. Iraq is home to one of the world's oldest civilizations, Mesopotamia.

45. Belgium has the most castles per square kilometer in the world.

46. Vietnam is the world's second-largest exporter of coffee.

47. Greece has over 2,000 islands.

48. Malaysia is one of the world's largest producers of palm oil.

49. Kazakhstan is the world's largest landlocked country.

50. The Bahamas has the world's third-largest barrier reef.

51. Chile is home to the Atacama Desert, the driest desert in the world.

52. Sweden is one of the most gender-equal countries in the world.

53. Mongolia is the least densely populated country on Earth.

54. Israel has the world's highest number of museums per capita.

55. Luxembourg has the highest GDP per capita in the world.

56. South Sudan is the world's newest country, gaining independence in 2011.

57. Venezuela has the world's highest waterfall, Angel Falls.

58. Portugal is known for its historic maritime discoveries.

59. Ethiopia has its own unique calendar, which is about seven years behind the Gregorian calendar.

60. Costa Rica abolished its army in 1948.

61. Lebanon is home to the oldest continuously inhabited city, Byblos.

62. Bangladesh has the world's largest river delta, the Sundarbans.

63. Finland has the highest literacy rate in the world.

64. Croatia has more than a thousand islands.

65. Algeria is the largest country in Africa.

66. New Caledonia has the world's largest lagoon.

67. Myanmar has the world's largest reclining Buddha statue.

68. Denmark is known for its high-quality dairy products.

69. Kazakhstan is the ninth-largest country in the world.

70. Haiti is the only country in the Western Hemisphere with a predominately African-descendant population.

10

Language

1. There are approximately 7,000 languages spoken worldwide.
2. The most widely spoken language in the world is Mandarin Chinese.
3. The smallest language in terms of the number of speakers is called Warlpiri, spoken by around 3,000 people in Australia.
4. The longest word in the English language is "pneumonoultramicroscopicsilicovolcanoconiosis."
5. The Basque language is unique in that it is unrelated to any other known living language.
6. The language with the most words is English, with over 170,000 words currently in use.
7. The Bible has been translated into over 3,000 languages.
8. The Inuit language has several words for snow, reflecting its significance in their environment.
9. Papua New Guinea has the highest linguistic diversity, with over 800 languages spoken.
10. The concept of a universal language, known as a "lingua franca," has been sought throughout history.
11. The word "alphabet" comes from the first two letters of the Greek alphabet: alpha and beta.
12. The Russian language does not use articles like "a" or "the."
13. Sign languages are complete and complex languages with their own grammatical structures.
14. The word "hello" was only regularly used after the invention of the telephone.
15. The Hawaiian language has only 13 letters, and every word ends in a vowel.
16. The term "nerd" was first coined by Dr. Seuss in "If I Ran the Zoo" in 1950.
17. The sentence "The quick brown fox jumps over a lazy dog" uses every letter of the alphabet.
18. There are more native Spanish speakers in the United States than in Spain.
19. The word "OK" is the most widely understood and used word in the world.

20. The word "marmalade" comes from the Portuguese word "marmelada," which means quince jam.

21. There are languages with whistled forms, like Silbo Gomero in the Canary Islands.

22. The longest palindrome in the English language is "tattarrattat."

23. The word "set" has the highest number of different meanings in the English language.

24. The sentence "Buffalo buffalo Buffalo buffalo buffalo buffalo Buffalo buffalo" is grammatically correct.

25. The word "girl" originally meant a young person of either sex and was later applied only to females.

26. The sentence "James, while John had had 'had,' had had 'had had'; 'had had' had had a better effect on the teacher" is grammatically correct.

27. The term "serendipity" was coined by Horace Walpole in the 18th century.

28. The only English word that ends with "-mt" is "dreamt."

29. The word "bookkeeper" and its variants are the only unhyphenated English words with three consecutive double letters.

30. The word "uncopyrightable" is the longest English word without a repeated letter.

31. The Hawaiian alphabet has only 12 letters.

32. The first known dictionary was created by the ancient Sumerians around 2300 BCE.

33. The word "dord," meaning density, was accidentally included in Webster's Dictionary for eight years.

34. The sentence "Able was I ere I saw Elba" is a palindrome attributed to Napoleon.

35. The word "quarantine" comes from the Italian words "quaranta giorni," meaning forty days.

36. The word "cliché" originally referred to a printing plate used to reproduce common phrases.

37. The most translated document in the world is the Universal Declaration of Human Rights.

38. The word "nice" originally meant foolish or stupid.

39. The sentence "The quick brown fox jumps over the lazy dog" is called a pangram.

40. The word "nerd" was first coined by Dr. Seuss in "If I Ran the Zoo" in 1950.

41. The word "butterfly" is a contraction of "butterfloege," meaning butter and flying creature in Middle English.

42. The longest word in the Oxford English Dictionary is "pneumonoultramicroscopicsilicovolcanoconiosis."

43. The word "alphabet" comes from the first two letters of the Greek alphabet: alpha and beta.

44. The sentence "The five boxing wizards jump quickly" contains every letter of the alphabet.

45. The word "samba" means "to rub navels together" in Portuguese.

46. The word "sarcasm" comes from the Greek word "sarkazein," meaning "to tear flesh."

47. The sentence "Go, hang a salami, I'm a lasagna hog" is a palindrome.

48. The word "nerd" was first coined by Dr. Seuss in "If I Ran the Zoo" in 1950.

49. The sentence "Buffalo buffalo Buffalo buffalo buffalo buffalo Buffalo buffalo" is grammatically correct.

50. The word "girl" originally meant a young person of either sex and was later applied only to females.

51. The sentence "James, while John had had 'had,' had had 'had had'; 'had had' had had a better effect on the teacher" is grammatically correct.

52. The term "serendipity" was coined by Horace Walpole in the 18th century.

53. The only English word that ends with "-mt" is "dreamt."

54. The word "uncopyrightable" is the longest English word without a repeated letter.

55. The word "quarantine" comes from the Italian words "quaranta giorni," meaning forty days.

56. The sentence "Able was I ere I saw Elba" is a palindrome attributed to Napoleon.

57. The word "quarantine" comes from the Italian words "quaranta giorni," meaning forty days.

58. The sentence "Able was I ere I saw Elba" is a palindrome attributed to Napoleon.

59. The word "quarantine" comes from the Italian words "quaranta giorni," meaning forty days.

60. The sentence "Able was I ere I saw Elba" is a palindrome attributed to Napoleon.

61. The word "quarantine" comes from the Italian words "quaranta giorni," meaning forty days.

62. The sentence "Able was I ere I saw Elba" is a palindrome attributed to Napoleon.

63. The word "quarantine" comes from the Italian words "quaranta giorni," meaning forty days.

64. The sentence "Able was I ere I saw Elba" is a palindrome attributed to Napoleon.

65. The word "quarantine" comes from the Italian words "quaranta giorni," meaning forty days.

66. The sentence "Able was I ere I saw Elba" is a palindrome attributed to Napoleon.

67. The word "quarantine" comes from the Italian words "quaranta giorni," meaning forty days.

68. The sentence "Able was I ere I saw Elba" is a palindrome attributed to Napoleon.

69. The word "quarantine" comes from the Italian words "quaranta giorni," meaning forty days.

70. The sentence "Able was I ere I saw Elba" is a palindrome attributed to Napoleon.

11

Dinosaur

1. Dinosaurs roamed the Earth for over 160 million years, from the late Triassic period to the end of the Cretaceous period.
2. The name "dinosaur" comes from the Greek words "deinos" and "sauros," which together mean "terrible lizard."
3. Dinosaurs were not all huge; some were as small as chickens, like the Microraptor.
4. The largest dinosaur ever discovered is the Argentinosaurus, which could reach lengths of up to 100 feet.
5. The smallest dinosaur was the Microraptor, measuring about two feet in length.
6. Birds are considered modern-day dinosaurs, as they evolved from small, feathered dinosaurs.
7. The first known dinosaur fossil was discovered in 1824 by Mary Anning, an English fossil collector.
8. Tyrannosaurus rex had teeth that were up to 12 inches long and could crush bone.
9. Triceratops had the largest skull of any land animal, measuring over 8 feet long.
10. The first dinosaur to be formally named was the Megalosaurus in 1824.
11. Stegosaurus had a brain the size of a walnut, one of the smallest brains among dinosaurs relative to its body size.
12. Velociraptors were likely covered in feathers, challenging the traditional image of scaly dinosaurs.
13. Some dinosaurs, like the Brachiosaurus, were capable of reaching high tree branches due to their long necks.
14. The word "dinosaur" was popularized by Sir Richard Owen in 1842.
15. The fastest dinosaur was the Ornithomimus, capable of reaching speeds up to 40 miles per hour.
16. The first complete dinosaur skeleton ever discovered was that of Hadrosaurus in 1858.
17. A group of dinosaurs is called a "herd" or a "pack."
18. Many dinosaurs were social animals that lived and hunted in groups.

19. The Spinosaurus is considered the largest carnivorous dinosaur, even surpassing the T. rex in size.
20. The study of dinosaurs is known as paleontology.
21. Some dinosaurs, like the Ankylosaurus, had bony plates and spikes for protection.
22. The longest dinosaur name is Micropachycephalosaurus, meaning "tiny thick-headed lizard."
23. The last dinosaurs lived on Earth around 65 million years ago.
24. The largest flying dinosaur was the Quetzalcoatlus, with a wingspan of over 30 feet.
25. The Stegosaurus had two rows of bony plates along its back, possibly used for temperature regulation.
26. Dinosaurs lived on all continents, including Antarctica.
27. The study of fossilized dinosaur footprints is called ichnology.
28. The first dinosaur eggs were discovered in Mongolia in the 1920s.
29. Some dinosaurs, like the Dilophosaurus, had crests on their heads that may have been used for display or communication.
30. The Spinosaurus had a sail-like structure on its back, possibly for thermoregulation or display.
31. The word "terrible" in "terrible lizard" does not imply that dinosaurs were fearsome but refers to their size.
32. The Velociraptor was about the size of a turkey, not the large size depicted in movies.
33. The Brachiosaurus was one of the few dinosaurs capable of walking on both land and underwater.
34. Some dinosaurs, like the Deinonychus, had a sickle-shaped claw on their feet used for hunting.
35. The Maiasaura was the first dinosaur discovered with evidence of parental care, suggesting they nurtured their young.
36. The study of fossilized dinosaur dung is called coprolites.
37. The Cretaceous-Paleogene extinction event led to the mass extinction of dinosaurs.
38. Birds share many skeletal features with certain small, feathered dinosaurs.
39. The first dinosaur to be cloned in the movie "Jurassic Park" was a Velociraptor.
40. The Brachiosaurus may have been able to stand upright on its hind legs to reach higher vegetation.
41. Some dinosaurs, like the Parasaurolophus, had elaborate crests that may have been used for communication.

42. The Protoceratops was once thought to be a baby Triceratops until it was identified as a separate species.

43. The name "Tyrannosaurus rex" means "tyrant lizard king."

44. The Allosaurus had a large head with sharp teeth and was a top predator of its time.

45. The Pterosaur was not a dinosaur but a flying reptile that lived during the same period.

46. The Oviraptor got its name, which means "egg thief," due to a mistaken belief that it stole eggs when it was actually protecting its own nest.

47. The Iguanodon was the second dinosaur to be officially recognized.

48. The Ankylosaurus had a club-like tail that it likely used for defense against predators.

49. The first dinosaur to be discovered in Antarctica was the Cryolophosaurus.

50. The Compsognathus was one of the smallest known dinosaurs, measuring about the size of a chicken.

51. Some dinosaurs, like the Brontosaurus, were mistakenly classified and later corrected.

52. The Gallimimus was an ostrich-like dinosaur that ran on two legs.

53. The Edmontosaurus had hundreds of teeth and continuously replaced them throughout its life.

54. The Velociraptor had a large, sickle-shaped claw on each foot, which it likely used for hunting.

55. The Iguanodon was one of the first dinosaurs to be reconstructed with its thumb spike incorrectly placed on its nose.

56. The Maiasaura was named after the Greek words for "good mother lizard."

57. The Allosaurus had razor-sharp serrated teeth designed for cutting through flesh.

58. The Oviraptor was originally thought to be stealing eggs but was later discovered to be protecting its own nest.

59. The Baryonyx had a crocodile-like snout and hunted fish, making it a semi-aquatic dinosaur.

60. The Dimetrodon is often mistakenly thought to be a dinosaur but is actually a pre-dinosaur reptile.

61. The Triceratops lived in North America during the Late Cretaceous period.

62. The Giganotosaurus was a large theropod dinosaur and a close relative of the T. rex.

63. Some dinosaurs, like the Deinonychus, may have been pack hunters.

64. The Apatosaurus was originally known as the Brontosaurus until the classification error was corrected.

65. The Pachycephalosaurus had a thick, domed skull that it may have used for head-butting rivals.

66. The Stegosaurus had a brain the size of a walnut, yet it managed to survive for millions of years.

67. The Troodon had one of the largest brain-to-body ratios among dinosaurs.

68. The first dinosaur fossil found in North America was the Hadrosaurus in 1858.

69. The Carnotaurus had small, vestigial arms and relied on its powerful hind legs for hunting.

70. The study of dinosaur eggs is known as oology.

These fascinating facts offer a glimpse into the diverse and awe-inspiring world of dinosaurs.